# H.E.L.P.

## Healing & Encouraging Life Poems

## Khali Williams
'The Wise Original Poet'

# H.E.L.P.

## Healing & Encouraging Life Poems

### Khali Williams
'The Wise Original Poet'

CB publishing

© 2011

www.CB-Publishing.com

This is a book of original poetry based on the divinely inspired thoughts of Khali Williams.

# H.E.L.P *Healing & Encouraging Life Poems*

Published in the United States of America by CB Publishing LLC an imprint of ChosenButterfly Publishing LLC

WWW.CB-PUBLISHING.COM

PO BOX 515

MILLVILLE, NJ 08332

ISBN 978-0-983-16371-8

Second Edition Printing
Printed In the United States of America
October 2011

Collins Khali Williams
khaliwop@yahoo.com
Camden, NJ 08104
WWW.KHALI.CB-PUBLISHING.COM

# DEDICATION

First and foremost, I must dedicate this book to God as well as my beloved wife, without either, none of this would have been possible.

I would also like to dedicate this to my sons, daughter and extended family.

For those family members who are no longer with us, I write this book in honor of you.

Finally, to my *new* family, friends and all who support me... Thank you.

Love and Respect,
Khali Williams aka
'The Wise Original Poet'

# FOREWORD

H.E.L.P. Healing and Encouraging Life Poems is without a doubt, a timely release, for such a time as this. These are very trying times for so many people and I do believe H.E.L.P. will be the book to soothe the mind and soul.

This book absolutely does what it was meant to do, heal, motivate, encourage and strengthen its reader. H.E.L.P. is a timeless tool for all generations; most certainly a book that is worth the investment that will always yield you, a positive return over and over and over again! Enjoy!!!

**Pastor Carla J. Riley**
Founder of Freedom Reigns In This Place
Church of the Living God
Mt. Laurel, NJ

# Table of Contents

# MOMMY

My mother passed on when I was only thirteen

So being a motherless child, I know exactly what that means

My love and respect to all mothers who take good care of their children

If they had to save them, they would run up in a burning building

All the single mothers who raise the children on their own

because the man who was supposed to be a king left his throne

All the strong mothers who do the best they can

To teach a young boy how to be a man

Mothers who show a young girl how to be a classy, respectable, woman

and a good wife

This is not just a Mother's Day poem but a celebration of mommy's life

To you, mom, this is my tribute, with care and an honorable salute

You will always be the strongest part of the tree; our root

When you did things it was not just to be seen

You were our true royal queen

So smart, so sweet, so nice

I pray you're with the Lord in paradise

## Real Fathers

I'm talking about real fathers, real men

The kind you don't have to ask for something over and over again

They refrain from the major sin

They operate under God's guidance with discipline

Head of house hold; King of the throne

Willing to work their fingers to the bone

Real fathers will make mistakes but don't mind being corrected

Their main job is to make sure the family is safe, secure,

and protected

We keep God first and then avoid the worse

Breaking every generational curse

Treating everyone with kindness, respect and love

Those are the qualities that Real men;

Real fathers are made of

# LOST CHILD

There is no worse pain then when you lose someone you love

But when it's your child your heart can smile to know they got

called from up above

It's okay to cry, but don't ask why

Just know they became a star in the sky

Think about the good times God let you share

The way you loved them and showed you cared

When you look up at night

you see him shining bright

You just ask the Lord can you see their face again

To please open up heavens doors and let you in

For now you thank Him and always pray

Your baby didn't die, they went peacefully away

# TRIBUTE TO BLACK WOMEN

When God created Adam and saw he was alone

He then created Eve from Adam's rib bone

She was his same color; his skin tone

I chose a woman the same color as me

My sisters you are the true queens of this civilization

May paradise be your destination

You are a black man's true sensation

For far too long you have been neglected and disrespected

Just for you this poem was selected

Together we have always prayed

You're a beautiful day that came to me and stayed

They try to compare you to the wind

but you're just so far beyond measure

A black woman is the true meaning of the word pleasure

You have the keys to unlock the doors of heaven

Call you my six day some say He made seven

You have the aroma of flowers, the freshness of rain

My love grows every hour and blessings I always gain

Black lady continue to hold your head high

I know very hard you will always try

You're the type of woman who is so very proud

Forever your face will stand out in a crowd

Black girl keep striving to do your best

I place you so far above the rest

# Khali Williams

To me you are the cream of the crop

Forever you will be at the tip of the top

"Keep on shining just like a diamond,"

This is what I say

You don't have to hear it from Simon

Black woman, stand by your black man's side

Together you both will never be denied

Understanding is something that you know

Everyday your knowledge and wisdom will grow.

Always in front and never behind

With you strength is so easy to find

If beauty was a second you would be an hour

Black woman you possess all the power

To me you are the sweetest of fruit

And for you, there will never be a substitute

So to you, black women, this is my tribute

For all my righteous sisters so much respect is due

I deeply and completely love the heaven out of you

If you should ever slip and began to fall down

I'm one black man, who will catch you before you hit the ground

From the cellar of my heart to the ceiling of my mind

They can search this whole universe and will still never find

a woman, better than a black woman this I feel is true

Almighty God has blessed me with you

# WEDDING POEM

Just for your intentions He began blessing you at the crack of dawn

And after you say "I do" He will continue to pour blessings on

There is a punishment for those who don't get married and do wrong

But for those who get married and do right the reward is very strong

Remember Cain went out in the wilderness and found a wife

When you go out and find someone they will change your life

God said man should not be alone

A king needs a queen to share his throne

Every day of marriage will not be peaches and cream

But after any nightmare you will have sweet dreams

Love is a work in progress

Give it your all and do your best

Then let the Lord Almighty handle the rest

# COFFEE

My baby told me she heard me do a lot of poems for other people

and when I do one for her it better not be no equal

She said when I do one for her it better be off the hook

So I went to my Lord asking permission to use words from His Holy book

He said a man who finds a wife finds a good thing

Well I found me an angel

and I feel heaven every time she spreads her wings

Just seeing her smile I can't describe how much joy she brings

She is the flesh of my flesh, bones of my bones

With her in my life I'll never be alone

If I had all the trees on earth as my pens and all the water as my ink

they would all run out and dry up

before the chain of my love breaks a link

This marriage will have no divorce

May God allow it to run its full course

That means until death do we part

So I write this with blood from my heart

Lord knows my words and feelings are true

The definition of real good love is *you*

My life has been full of lessons from each one of them I have learned

I thank God for all of my blessings and for me finally getting my turn

To have someone who is worth living for

A real man can't ask for anything more

Today the heavens have opened up

and I *finally* got real good coffee in my cup

# POWER OF PLANTS

Almighty God has given man power over all living things

over the animals, over other people, and

over the plants that are in the ground

But man has fallen down, and the plants have power over us now

There's a plant called Marijuana, Haze and Weed

I call it some smoke that can cause you to no longer succeed

Urine dirty for more then thirty days, spending money all kinds of ways

Easily losing their job or either getting robbed

The next plant is one I truly hate because it's legal

and it does not discriminate.

It don't care about your race, gender, or age

It has so many people listed in the obituary page

The people be fiending for days

Looking on the ground digging in ash trays

Even the so called smart people it has in a choke hold

I've seen doctors and lawyers standing out in the wet and cold

You don't have to guess you already know

I'm talking about that nasty plant called tobacco

The next one is a mental thief; it comes from the coca leaf

When they add baking soda and hot water it turns in to crack cocaine

It makes people lose their mind and all their brain

Mothers abandon their hungry child

Khali Williams

and they run the streets crazy and wild

This next one is last but certainly not least

I watch it turn beauty into a beast

It makes them steal, lie, and be full of greed

derived from the poppy plant and seed.

Makes their arms and hands swell like gloves

No longer able to hold on to the things they love

Like Bob with no hope, neck stuck out waiting for the rope

Because they are addicted to that dope

Ready to kill or con because of that heroin

I pray that my people can return to the status of giants

Not low on the ground like ants

Then take the power back away from the plants.

# ABORT

God said give this message clear with no distortion

The number one killer of African Americans is abortion

Started after slavery with a company name Eugenics

Now changed the name to Planned Parenthood clinics

In every ghetto and inner city with easy access

Modern day genocide at its best

You may have thought it was AIDS, heart disease, or violence

But the killers are out in the open and working in silence

May the Lord give us victory to defeat them and win

Against this organization that commits such great sin

Politics say the woman should have her choice

What about the children

who never get a chance to use their voice?

Do your own research then you will be able to tell

all of those who started it, support it, and work for it

Should be afraid of hell

# KHALI VS SATAN

Just because I'm from Camden doesn't mean I have to live a life of
crime, sin, and shame
So I ask Almighty God could I challenge the devil to a game
He said, "Son, you have my lessons to take him down,
you are a king so reclaim your crown."
Old Satan began to laugh and said, "Khali you are a joke,
I took on stronger men than you and they all ended up broke."
I knew the devil was a coward who would not play me alone
So he started dialing down on his hell phone
he called *hate, liar, greed* and *kill*
These spirits would rejoice every time innocent blood would spill
Then I called up to heaven for the very best
The ones who have already passed the test
I called *Truth, Faith, Belief* and *Love*
These are the qualities that a real team is made of
The devil cheated from the opening tip and got the ball first
But what else can you expect I'm playing against the very worst
The game was back and forth very close
Each team thinking they would win by the most
With time about to run out, Satan scored a three
but that only put them up by two.
My team looked at me and said, "Khali, what you gonna do?"

# Khali Williams

So I went hard to the basket up for a slam dunk.

Satan scratched me across my eyes, "I said you no good punk."

With that evil grin, he said, "Now if you want to win,

you have to make it at the foul line

but you can't now, you are totally blind."

Faith said, "Khali, we have faith in you."

Belief said, "We believe in you too."

Truth said, "You are the truth, now show him the proof."

Love said, "Every one close your eyes," and we prayed,

"This is God's team, God's city; the shot will be made."

The next thing I heard was my city scream and yell

That let me know the shot had fell Now I can lock that devil in the

bottom of hell

Never ever again will he cause crime and violence

In the city of Camden

# DESTINY IS CALLING

My destiny is calling me out of the pit

So I refuse to quit

No longer will I just stand still

Brick by brick my life I'm going to rebuild

I've had a spiritual rebirth

I'm a child of God so I know what I'm worth

This present situation is not it

My destiny is calling me out of my pit

I won't be locked down mentally, financially, or emotionally

My faith in the Lord has set me free

No more arguing, fighting, or yelling

No more drug using, drug dealing, or selling

He erased the record of a convicted felon

Now it's only the good news I'm telling

So whenever you're ready and have the desire

He can bring you out of that fire

He has the power to help you rise

gives you discernment to take off the devil's disguise

You don't have to accept any more hits

Your destiny is calling you out of the pit

# EMBRACING THE CALL

I have heard them say, "Khali, you missed your calling."

That made me feel like I was an angel that had fallen

So now I have to embrace my call

that means no more umbrella when the

rain starts to fall

Answering the phone when the needy start to call

But God gives me the wisdom to know I can't help them all

So I began to listen with my heart, mind, soul and spirit

The message was loud and clear and I could hear it

Treat everyone with respect and always tell them the truth

And for those who don't believe I have The Book as my proof

But the others you will have to take them high up on a roof

and show them that sin is the same as if they were to jump off

'Cause everyday won't be sweet and soft

Sometimes you will cry and need a paper cloth

Once you have become a part of the Lord's elite team

It's now your duty to help others fulfill their dreams

It's the God in you, the God in me, the God that's always around

He helps us get up when we fall down

Embracing the call is obeying that heavenly sound

# HUSTLER

You're no hustler

You don't know what hustling is

All you know how to do is get some of hers and some of his

Let me tell you about real hustlers those who have jobs

Not the ones on the street trying to deal, steal, kill and rob

We don't have no problem with punching the clock

We're not hugging the block selling dope, pills and rocks

Waiting to be the next one to get locked

We are dedicated to our family can't leave them at night cold and lonely

Real hustlers are educated and know how to get money

More than one way has it coming in every two weeks, every week, or

every day

and even have some put up for a raining day.

It's called a 401k or IRA.

We don't waste our money shooting dice or playing cards,

buying diamonds, ice, and hot cars.

We have it invested so it can double twice and go far.

Real hustlers don't talk they get the job done.

I was blessed to go to court to get custody of my son.

There is one more thing I have to say

for all of you fake hustlers I bow my head and pray.

# GARDEN OF GETHSEMANE

Pressing through the Garden of Gethsemane

To reach my destiny

No stressing, feelings not hardened

I know where I'm supposed to be

With faith and understanding it's not always easy but it must be done

It is the will of the Almighty One

Who created everything in, on, under, and above this earth

I'm a child of His, I know what I'm worth

If you believe in the power of what He can do

Then there is nothing or no one that can ever stop you

We must continue to do our part

We all must open up our heart

He gave you a gift and some skills

We believers have a Kingdom to build!

It's inside of you as well as me

Keep pressing through the Garden of Gethsemane to your

Destiny

# DRESS TO KILL

Every day you must stay suited, helmeted and booted

Shield and sword included

Dress to kill

Ready to do God's will

Either you deal or no deal

The enemy never takes time off

he wants to catch you relaxed and soft

Sleeping with your eyes closed

That's when he punches you in the mouth and bloodies your nose

He makes you think it's wrong to get a divorce, but God said abuse

and pain should never be your course

Also tells you don't punish your children

But if you spare the rod, you spoil the child, they need discipline

So they can learn to fear sin

Now you have on your armor, reading and prayer is your bullet

proof vest

No need to worry, no need to guess, you have been favored and

blessed

You were given the wisdom knowing when to move, when to be still

Every day you must stay Dressed to Kill

# AWAKEN MY SISTERS

Awaken my sister, no more time to rest

He is calling you He wants your best

All that you have been through was only a test

No more time to sleep

Stop wasting time counting sheep

You are ready to go in deep

Where others have refused to go

because they really don't know who is running the show

He wants you to use your gift

There are so many that you can uplift

A lot of people are spiritually stuck on thrift

You must have the desire to encourage and inspire

Warn them about the fire

You have the choice to go left or right

Early in the day or late at night

Either peacefully or with a fight

Never go with an empty cup

You must pray, you must read, you must move

You Must Wake Up

# CHANGING OF THE GUARD

Where are the Joshuas for the changing of the guard?

There are not that many

because the training is hard

But God said He places no burden on us that we can't handle

He gave us Basic Instructions Before Leaving Earth.

That spells Bible; a Holy Manual

Now all of you will not listen

A lot will be missing

But we still must keep on fishing

So that the next generation will have the necessary information

To reach their destination

The believers have to do a lot more

than what was done before

Our actions and words should be our credit card

Like Joshua, we must prepare for the changing of the guard

## FREE TO SOAR

I'm like an eagle free to soar

I'm like a lion not afraid to roar

I'm a man of God always on tour

Spreading the Good News and true Word

To those who have been abused, and have not yet heard

About the power that can forgive and heal

It can change the way you think and how you feel

Those who have faith know it's real spiritually and mentally

I'm free no hand cuffs or shackles on me

Whatever the devil tries to lock

My Lord has given me the key

I can fly with my new wings up so high

I'll hear the angels sing

Going places I have never been before

Can't rest, Can't sleep, Can't snore

I thank God I'm free to soar

## ON FIRE FOR LORD

It easy to be on fire for the Lord

The price is free that's a cost we all can afford

Remember when you were on fire for the devil?

You would go to very low levels

The excuse was then I was young, sexy, and hot

So after the club you was in the after hour spot.

Now you want a different kind of fire

The type that takes your soul much higher

Makes all the believers admire, and the unbelievers desire

It's time to start using your gift, talent, and skill

Making good decision with your free will

By letting scriptures pile up in your heart like wood

Then set yourself on fire and do some good

Don't take this life for all fun and games

Don't be amongst the unbelievers in the hell flames

When we touch and agree, then say, "Yes" with a head nod

From that point on we will be on fire for God

# PERFECTING MY PURPOSE

As I perfect my purpose it puts me in pursuit of my perfection

It's mandatory I seek God's protection.

He points me in the right direction

When I close my eyes I see His face

I can feel I'm in the right place

I have the best lawyer on my case

My examples are the prophets who were appointed

They let me know who is and who is not anointed

Therefore I won't be misled or disappointed

I continue to pray, continue to stay far, far away

From those who think God's work is a joke and play

They always talking and guessing because they don't

Understand about favor and blessings

They were not in pursuit of perfection

I thank Him my walk is correct

My purpose He perfects

# <u>ALREADY DONE</u>

It's already done its already complete

You were made with love and care, soft and sweet

You were created and built to last long

You know when to be firm and when to be strong

Thank God you were designed to perfection

One of His best selections

When He does a thing He does it right

He gave you a natural glow that even shines at night

Only you can add on and not let anyone subtract

That means you can never be a pawn

But a queen who can attack

Taking care of yourself, husband, family, and making it fun

You are second to none

God said "It is Already Done"

# ONLY ONE

All I can do is thank you for everything I feel

It lets me know you are real

Thank you for the air I breathe

You are the one who relieves

I thank you for the food I eat

Lord to me you've been so sweet

Even for the rain every drop takes away the pain; makes it stop

Even when I close my eyes my insight

Lets me understand why

Nobody can count every star

That proves who you are

I watch the glow of the moon

and I can tell you're coming soon

Every day I feel the warmth of the sun;

I know in my soul and spirit

You are the Only One.

# MISSION

Thank you Lord for this position

you have giving me spiritual intuition

righteousness, I know the definition

Forever I will be on a mission

I get on my knee and thank thee

For giving me the ability to catch one drop of rain

and stretch it into a river;

whisper one word to people's brain; cause your whole body to shiver

I feel I can hold the sun in my hand so I can lead the way

give it to God's people so they can shine every day

Carry the moon on my back and take it for a ride

some say, "Khali you proud."

No, it's the devil who deals with pride

Almighty God has given me a job I must carry it out

bringing back yesterday

so you will know what tomorrow is about

I'm always striving to change my condition

Placing me and my family in a better position

I stay fully loaded scripture be my ammunition

I'm one of God's soldiers and killing the devil is my mission

I continue to pray that He allows me to walk on water and part open the

sea save my people from drowning

by setting them free.

Return sight to the blind. I want the deaf to hear

# Khali Williams

If you knew like I knew you would show a little more fear

Let's get the homeless off the street

Give the hungry something to eat

Bring some heat to the ones who are cold

Can these people have some hope to hold?

All of these things can so easily be done

With sincere faith in the True and Living One

I need each and every one to stop, look, listen, and pray

for me to be successful on my mission. Ever since the first day

I started to crawl to the last day when I finally fall

Everyday I'm going to give Him my absolute all

I made up my mind this is my most important decision

Forever I will be on a mission

Serving my Lord

I will be on a mission

This is my reward

I will be on a mission

Doing God's will.

I will be on a mission,

I refuse to stand still.

Forever I will be on a mission

To Him all praises are due.

God Bless, Peace & I love each one of you.


Khali 'The Wise Original Poet' Williams

# ABOUT KHALI WILLIAMS
## 'The Wise Poet'

$\mathcal{A}$ life that could have continued going down a bad road, ended up being a testament to how the Lord is willing and able to answer prayers and change lives. Khali Williams was born and raised in Camden, New Jersey one of the roughest cities in America. He lost his mother at the young age of thirteen years old, which further complicated his life. Wanting to have a better life for himself, Khali enlisted into the United States Army where he spent 2 years as a paratrooper.

Upon coming back to Camden Khali unfortunately slipped into a lifestyle of crime and spent many years of incarceration because of it. It was hearing the news that his son's mother was on drugs and not taking care of him that caused Khali to cry out to the Lord. He specifically asked the Lord for his freedom, to help him turn from a life of crime and to grant him custody of his son.

In August 1999, the Lord began answering those prayers and Khali was released from jail. A couple of months later he was blessed with temporary employment which soon became full-time permanent employment. Khali has been on his job for over twelve years now and was blessed to have been honored with Employee of the Year.

One year after being released from jail, Khali was granted sole custody of his son. He has used his experiences to teach his son and as a result his son is continuing to walk down the right path.

A few years ago, Khali prayed and asked the Lord to send him a God fearing wife. The Lord answered that prayer and sent a former childhood sweetheart named Shirley back into his life. They became united in marriage on Valentine's Day 2009.

It was at Khali's wife's monthly fellowships that he met Ayanna Clark, CEO of CB Publishing. The Lord moved upon Ayanna's heart to assist Khali in publishing his first book. *H.E.L.P Healing and Encouraging Life Poems.*

What you are holding in your hand is proof that God is able to change lives, establish divine connections and most importantly answer prayers beyond our wildest dreams!

# CONTACT INFORMATION

Khali can be contacted via:

**E-mail:** khaliwop@yahoo.com

**Website:** www.**khali.cb-publishing**.com

**Phone:** 856-625-1435

Thank you for your support.

www.ingramcontent.com/pod-product-compliance
Lightning Source LLC
Chambersburg PA
CBHW051711090426

42736CB00013B/2642